Thanks,
Daryl Johnson

The Writing's on the Wall for all Mankind to See

DAWN JOHNSON

authorHOUSE®

AuthorHouse™
1663 Liberty Drive, Suite 200
Bloomington, IN 47403
www.authorhouse.com
Phone: 1-800-839-8640

First published by AuthorHouse 9/24/2008

ISBN: 978-1-4343-8579-6 (sc)

Scripture Quotations are taken from the King James Version of the Bible.

Library of Congress Control Number: 2008908421

Printed in the United States of America
Bloomington, Indiana

This book is printed on acid-free paper.

In Loving Memory of
DorothyLu Henry!

Table of Contents

For all my readers

This book is a compilation of inspirational passages and short stories. Read and expect God to show up in your life, and know that God loves you, and so do I. If you do not know Christ, my hope is that this book will minister to your soul so that you will get saved today! My gift to the world is the gift that God has blessed me with—*The Writing's on the Wall for All Mankind to See* (Daniel 5:1–6, 13–31).

Acknowledgments

First and foremost, I give all the honor and glory to my Lord and Savior Jesus Christ, who blessed me with this wonderful gift to share with others. Thanks to my church family, TLC ministry, and Bishop Kevia F. Elliott, whose preached word brought me closer to the cross every day. Thanks to my family, who supported me day and night. There are too many to name—much love. Thanks to Kenneth Franklin Jr. for all your help. Thanks to Cheryl Williams, my stylist, for all your support. Thanks to my dad, Walter Reed Sr. I love you. Thanks to my sister, JoAnn Dow, who critiqued my work with honesty and love. Your blessings are on the way. Special thanks to my mother, Mary Wilson, for believing in me when at times I didn't think I could do it. I love you. Thanks to my children, Shayla Lee, Kayla Johnson, and Gabriella Johnson, who gave me space to write without realizing it. I love you all. To my husband, Clayton Johnson, I thank you for your support and your words of encouragement. We share a love that goes above and beyond the test of time. I love you!

Daniel 5:1–6, 13–31: "BELSHAZZAR the king made a great feast to a thousand of his lords, and drank wine before the thousand. Belshazzar, whiles he tasted the wine, commanded to bring the golden and silver vessels which his father Nebuchadnezzar had taken out of the temple which was in Jerusalem; that the king, and his princes, his wives, and his concubines, might drink therein. Then they brought the golden vessels that were taken out of the temple of the house of God which was at Jerusalem; and the king, and his princes, his wives, and his concubines, drank in them. They drank wine, and praised the gods of gold, and of silver, of brass, of iron, of wood, and of stone. In the same hour came forth fingers of a man's hand, and wrote over against the candlestick upon the plaister of the wall of the king's palace: and the king saw the part of the hand that wrote. Then the king's countenance was changed, and his thoughts troubled him, so that the joints of his loins were loosed, and his knees smote one against another…Then was Daniel brought in before the king. And the king spake and said unto Daniel, Art thou that Daniel, which art of the children of the captivity of Judah, whom the king my father brought out of Jewry? I have even heard of thee, that the spirit of the gods is in thee, and that light and understanding and excellent wisdom is found in thee. And now the wise men, the astrologers, have been brought in before me, that they should read this writing, and make known unto me the interpretation thereof: but they could not shew the interpretation of the thing: And I have heard of thee, that thou canst make interpretations, and dissolve doubts: now if thou canst read the writing, and make known to me the interpretation thereof, thou shalt be clothed with scarlet, and have a chain of gold about thy neck, and shalt be the third ruler in the kingdom. Then Daniel answered and said before the king, Let thy gifts be to thyself, and give thy rewards to another; yet I will read the writing unto the king, and make known to him the interpretation. O thou king, the most high God gave Nebuchadnezzar thy father a kingdom, and majesty, and glory, and honour: And for the majesty that he gave him, all people, nations, and languages, trembled and feared before him: whom he would he slew; and whom he would he kept alive; and whom he would he set up; and whom he would he put down. But when his heart was lifted up, and his mind hardened in pride, he was deposed from his kingly throne, and they took his glory from him: And he was driven from the sons of men; and his heart was made like the beasts, and his dwelling was with the wild asses: they fed him with grass like oxen, and his body was wet with the dew of heaven; till he knew that the most high God ruled in the kingdom of men, and that he appointeth over it whomsoever he will. And thou his son, O Belshazzar, hast not humbled thine heart, though thou knewest all this; But hast lifted up thyself against the LORD of heaven; and they have brought the vessels of his house before thee, and thou, and thy lords, thy wives, and thy concubines, have drunk wine in them; and thou hast praised the gods of silver, and gold, of brass, iron, wood, and stone, which see not, nor hear, nor know: and the God in whose hand thy breath is, and whose are all thy ways, hast thou not glorified: Then was the part of the hand sent from him; and this writing was written. And this is the writing that was written, MENE, MENE, TEKEL, UPHARSIN. This is the interpretation of the thing: MENE; God hath numbered thy kingdom, and finished it. TEKEL; Thou art weighed in the balances, and art found wanting. PERES; Thy kingdom is divided, and given to the Medes and Persians. Then commanded Belshazzar, and they clothed Daniel with scarlet, and put a chain of gold about his neck, and made a proclamation concerning him, that he should be the third ruler in the kingdom. In that night was Belshazzar the king of the Chaldeans slain. And Darius the Median took the kingdom, being about threescore and two years old."

1 Peter 4:17: "For the time is come that judgment must begin at the house of God: and if it first begin at us, what shall the end be of them that obey not the gospel of God?"

Chapter I
"Saving Grace"

The Believers' Club

Join the Believers' Club today, for tomorrow is not promised. Once you join, you are a member for life. No one can cancel your membership or even vote you out. The best part is that this club is free. There is no admission charge and no application fee. You can't beat the hours, and the dress code is "come as you are." All you need to do is show up with a readiness and a willingness to receive. "Receive what?" you ask. *The word of God.* The Believers' Club operates by faith and promotes love. Once you are in God's presence, you will notice a change. Your hands and feet will look new, but check out your heart, because that is different too. You can invite as many friends as you like, but I must warn you that the word sometimes bites. Crying and shouting is a part of praise and worship, but casting stones is not part of our service. Are you ready to move higher every day of your life? Or do you *still* need to ponder on what's wrong and what's right? God promises to *never* leave you alone. Enough said. Come and make heaven your home!

Acts 2:21: "And it shall come to pass, that whosoever calls on the name of the Lord shall be saved."

Sold Out

The sign on the door says, "Closed, gone for today." You look at your watch and rush right away. You are hoping to make the store down the street, because it is the only place left to buy the chocolates you eat. *Just made it!* You walk in the door prepared to buy your favorites. You look at the counter and realize they're all gone.

"Sold out ten minutes ago," the man yells from behind you.

You look at him strangely and say, "That can't be. I rushed to get here, so there must be at least three."

"No! There are none," the man replies. "You can come back tomorrow, and I hope you are on time."

The very next day when you are leaving for church, you notice two accidents but continue to rush. You pull into the parking lot, hitting the brakes. *Just made it!* You walk in the door and start to look around. No seats are available for you to sit down. You look at your watch and realize the time. You are five minutes late, still running behind. As you stand in the back, you hear the pastor say, "Salvation is yours. Receive it today!" With everyone praying, you know you should move, but something inside causes you to refuse. "Harden not your heart," you hear him say. "Come give your life to Christ, and get saved today!" As you walk down the aisle, it suddenly hits you. You made it on time for the best part of the service. Later that night, you get on your knees to pray and start to recall the events of the day. Many past emotions begin to resurface, but now you are sold out to Jesus to be used for his purpose.

> **Hebrews 4:16:** "Let us therefore come boldly unto the throne of grace, that we may obtain mercy, and find grace to help in time of need."

Reconstruction

I remember the time I lost my way and fell victim to captivity. Curled up in a fetal position, I lifted my hands and asked God for help. I asked him to help rebuild my life after I lost my dreams in the dry places of a desolate situation. Dust collected on my inspirational palette, and my only memories were of failure. I was slowly moving in a tunnel that constricted my passion into a box of disappointment. *Open the latch?* A familiar voice carried a message of hope and prosperity. The voice of God *instantly* restored and replenished my soul. Now the pen glides on the paper, and the words become more vivid. My plan is to take back everything that the enemy has stolen. The plan is to renew my mind daily with God's word. The Holy Bible is my tool to fight fear and depression. I am more than a conqueror girded with my loins about me. *Deliverance is here! Deliverance is here!*

Psalm 32:7: "Thou art my hiding place; thou shalt preserve me from trouble; thou shalt compass me about with songs of deliverance."

Car Trouble

Driving down a bleak road, my vehicle comes to an abrupt stop. I turn the key in the ignition and press my foot on the brake, but the car will not start. I am traveling from Southern Virginia to Maryland and just filled the gas tank about an hour ago. *Surely my car has not run out of gas.* I step out of the vehicle and proceed to lift the hood. I am looking for signs of overheating, but everything appears to be intact. I check the tires for tread separation, but everything looks fine.

I can call my mechanic and ask him if anything seems unusual, but the battery in my cell phone is dead. I left the charger on the table at home prior to my trip. *What do I do now?* This road looks abandoned, but if I wait it out, someone will come by. *One hour later.* That's strange—no travelers. Maybe if I walk up the road about two miles, I can find someone to help me.

Before leaving, I try to start the car, but the keys suddenly fall to the floor. I bend forward to retrieve them, when my ears start ringing and my nose starts to bleed. As I lift my head, the blood stains my shirt, and the ringing gets louder. *Did I hit something?*

I stumble out of the car with severe chest pains. I notice cuts on my arms and legs. *I don't recall ever starting the car.* I drag myself to the rear of the vehicle and notice that the car has moved from its original position. *Someone has just hit me.* I nervously look around but can't find anyone. My left taillight is broken, and the bumper is damaged. "Hello!" I call out. "Hello, is anyone there?" *No answer.*

I manage to pull myself up while holding tightly to the car door. The temperature outside drops below thirty degrees, and my nose won't stop bleeding. As I lay shivering in the back seat of my car, the loud ringing in my ears turn into voices. "Are you prepared to die?" the first voice asks. "Have you done everything in life that you needed to do?"

the second voice says. I bang my head on the leather upholstery in order to drown out the voices.

The third voice comes in crystal clear, "Have you given your life to Christ?" *I remember going to church with my mother a couple of times.* The third voice says, "Have you prayed the prayer of salvation?" *I have prayed many times to God for things that I wanted.* The first voice says, "Did you ask God to forgive you for your sins?" *Sins. Everyone sins.* The second voice says, "Do you believe that Jesus died for you and rose on the third day?" *I have lost my mind.*

"Help, is there anyone out there?" I wait for a reply, and then all three voices start talking in unison, "Stop running from me and listen to my voice. Salvation is the key to eternal life. Accept me today in your heart, and I will renew your mind. The blood you see is symbolic of the blood that Jesus shed on the cross for your sins. The pain is a portion of what Jesus endured while dying on the cross to save you. Acknowledge him as Lord and Savoir in your life today!"

The tears well up in my eyes, and I can feel a strong tug on my heart. I open my mouth and scream out, "*Yes*! *Yes*! Yes, I believe that Jesus was sent to save a sinner like me." I lift my hands in the air and exhale. My nose stops bleeding, and the chest pains are no longer evident. I look at my arms and legs and notice that the scars are still present. The sun has risen, and the morning air is cool. I move to the front seat and put the key in the ignition, and with anticipation, the car starts.

I ponder upon what happened and begin to ask God, "Why did you have me go through the pain only to allow my car to start afterward?" God answers me early that morning and says, "I had to get you to a place where you could only depend on me. I removed the pain, but left the scar, so that in times of trouble, you will remember where your help comes from. Weeping may endure for a night, but joy comes in the morning."

What is the lesson?
God is salvation!

Everything that happens to you in life is not by chance. In this story, the car breaks down, and the driver is injured by another vehicle that fails to stop. Sometimes our lives are so hectic that we try to keep going without realizing that we need to slow down and rest (Genesis 2:2–3).

God uses various situations to get our immediate attention. This is seen when the driver is unable to locate help or to use the cell phone. God does not want us to become dependent on anything other than him (Exodus 34:14). He wants us to love, honor, and obey him.

In the story, the driver is in pain and moves to the back seat to lie down. Have you noticed that when you humble yourself before the Lord, he will answer your prayers? It is in the back seat of the vehicle that the change takes place. The driver begins to hear three voices talking in unison, symbolizing the Trinity: God the Father, Son, and the Holy Spirit (Matthew 28:19). We need to stop making excuses for everything that goes wrong in our lives and start listening to God's voice.

God wants to deliver us from the hand of the enemy and welcome us into the house of worship. Notice once the driver accepts God into his or her life; we see that the situation turns around for good. The car starts, and God is forever remembered as the God of salvation (Isaiah 12:2)! If you do not have a personal relationship with God, then don't miss your opportunity to get to know him today!

Chapter II
"Running Scared"

Diagnosis

Have you been told that you have less than three months to live or that you will never give birth to kids? Do you hold your head down in shame because you are HIV positive? Or maybe you have been told the tumor in your body is cancerous. Are you willing to share your test results with your family and friends? Or do you question the doctor's judgment and wait for a second opinion. *What's your diagnosis?* Do you believe God can heal you from your pain? Your illness is only a test of your faith. Are you living each day of your life in fear? Stop doubting God's power, and start each day in prayer. Your trials and tribulations help to build your character. Always seek God's face and desire to be in his presence. Surrender to his will, and let God reveal the outcome.

> **Proverbs 3:5–6:** "Trust in the LORD with all thine heart; and lean not unto thine own understanding. In all thy ways acknowledge him, and he shall direct thy paths."

Intruder

You are gone for a night but return in the morning. You are terrified to find someone has broken into your home. The door is ajar, and the curtains are drawn back. You have uneasy feelings and start to panic. How long were you watched—*one week, two months, or maybe a year?* Strangers invaded the home you built. *Is it safe?* Look to God for answers, and wait for a response. Fear is not an option, nor is running away. God wants you to trust and exercise faith. God will replace all of your possessions and hold us accountable on the Day of Judgment. The day is coming when we must speak about our works and then accept God's verdict and suffer the consequences.

> **John 10:9–10:** "I am the door: by me if any man enter in, he shall be saved, and shall go in and out, and find pasture. The thief cometh not, but for to steal, and to kill, and to destroy: I am come that they might have life, and that they might have it more abundantly."

Lost Love

Heartache and disappointment are a heavy load to bear. You offered to carry the load instead of taking it to God in prayer. You reach out for someone to help bandage your wounds. But your cuts are so deep that even your friends *must* refuse. Your eyes are filled with tears of self-pity. So with each person you meet, a part of your heart goes missing. You bypass your *inner* feelings and forget to proceed with caution. Instead, you move forward, down a path of destruction. People say that they love you, and this makes you vulnerable. You never want to get hurt or end up alone. You desire to find your one *true* love—a love that knows no bounds and is always there to comfort. *So what's the good news?* God can restore your broken heart. He is a God of second chances. He specializes in fixing broken vessels and making them whole again.

> **Mark 12:30:** "And thou shalt love the Lord thy God with all thy heart, and with all thy soul, and with all thy mind, and with all thy strength: this is the first commandment."

Healing Rain

Drip! Drip! The rain bounces off the roof, hitting the solid concrete and forming large puddles on the ground. It starts out slow and then picks up speed rapidly. The roads are wet, and the leaves are soaking in a pile underneath the tree. The umbrella used for protection is torn into shreds and left discarded on the side of the road. Children and adults have vacated the premises, afraid of getting drenched from the rain. All but one has taken cover this day.

Today Lauren decides to leave her home to feel the cool rain against her skin. With so much on her mind, the rain comforts her and gives her freedom to be who she really is—a carefree, loving person. She runs through the puddles, playfully kicking the water into the air. Spinning with her arms outstretched, she feels no fear or rejection. She likes everything about herself.

The rain quickly falls on her face and lands on her eyelashes. Lauren blinks a couple of times to recover her eyesight. She notices that the rain on her face has turned warm and salty, no longer the cool, refreshing moisture she first encountered. Lauren's tears have begun to coincide with the rain, causing a melancholy mood. She fights the urge to run away and hide. Her emotions have been bottled up for so long that it's time to release her feelings, and what better place than outside in the pouring rain? There is no one around to hear her scream or even to see her tears fall freely down her cheeks.

Lauren began enjoying life at nine years old, when she became a member of the Baltimore Cheerleading Camp. This was a special time, when she could feel confident about herself. Weeks before a major competition, she would practice her gymnastics flips and tumbles three to four hours a day. The adrenaline rush she experienced on the first day of competition left her excited and honored. She was happy to be part of a team that taught young kids the importance of self-control and discipline. The coach would always say, "No pain, no gain," a statement that remains fresh in Lauren's mind.

After completing cheerleading camp, Lauren remembers going to live with her grandmother. Her grandmother, the primary caregiver, was always so strict. Unable to go to the mall or to the movies with her friends, Lauren felt trapped in a world of imprisonment. She wanted to have her freedom and spent many years rebelling against everyone.

She doesn't understand why her mother walked out on her, without a kiss or a card to say goodbye. *Maybe it was best this way—no words to exchange and no broken promises to make.* Lauren loved her mother dearly, and the thought of her leaving left Lauren bitter and skeptical about loving another person. Lauren's neck stiffens as she recalls losing the bracelet that her mother gave her to seal their union. Her mother's words are so clear. "Lauren, I will never leave you. You will always be my baby girl." *How much weight do these words carry now that she is gone?*

Lauren's father remarried shortly after her twenty-fourth birthday. He relocated out of state with his new wife, relinquishing all of his fatherly duties. With no one to talk to about her feelings, she grew depressed and often thought of ending her life. At age twenty-six, Lauren lives in a one-bedroom apartment, where she fights daily with emotional issues. She no longer wants to smile and pretend that everything in her life is fine but wants to reach out for someone, anyone, to save her from herself.

The rain relaxes her body and ministers to her soul. The sound of the rain is therapeutic, allowing her to drift into a place of peace. Her legs buckle, and she drops to her knees. Lauren watches as the water makes rippling effects around her. She belts out a loud laugh and begins pounding the concrete with her fists. *This is for leaving me! This is for not coming back to get me! This is for not loving me enough to call or even write!*

Minutes later a gentleman driving a grey Oldsmobile spots Lauren in the rain. He rushes over and kneels down beside her, placing both arms tightly around her. He can't imagine the frustration and hurt that she is feeling. He takes his coat off and spreads it gently around her shoulders. He softly whispers into her ear, "God loves you. He has not forgotten. Trust and believe that he will deliver you from your pain and anguish." He grabs both her fists and slowly loosens her fingers. With her hands completely open, he brings them together so that her palms are touching. The man says to Lauren, "Ask in Jesus' name, and it shall be given unto you."

What is the lesson?
God is peace!

Do you ever feel like you are alone? Does it seem as if no one cares about your feelings? God cares. In the story, we see that Lauren's mother and father have left the home. Lauren's grandmother is raising her based on her rules and standards. There are many children today who live in a one-parent household or who are being raised by other relatives. Do not let this stop you from succeeding in life (Psalm 27:10). There is no reason to hide, because God has placed you in a perfect position for healing.

We see that Lauren feels abandoned and uses the rain as a means of escape from her pain. But isn't it good to know that God will never forsake us (Deuteronomy 31:6)? We can always talk with him and find peace in our circumstances. He hears us when we pray and sends others to help us in our time of need. In the story, we see the guy driving the Oldsmobile instructing Lauren to pray (Luke 11:1–4). He doesn't know anything about Lauren's situation, but he knows that there is power in prayer.

There may be times in our lives when we don't know what to pray for. If that is the case, then we are to ask God for wisdom and guidance. His word is truth and speaks restoration into our lives (Isaiah 39:8). Although Lauren was confused about her life, she was willing to receive help. We must put pride aside for God to minister healing into our souls and love into our hearts.

Chapter III
"Imprisonment"

Dark Room

Does your past have you trapped in despair? Do the shadows that chase you into the corner overtake you behind closed doors? Do you never love yourself enough, and are you always trying to fit in? You promised yourself you would never go back to *that* dark room. Yet you are always looking for others to validate who you are. *Who does God say you are?* But the world keeps calling you, stretching forth its cold hands. The enemy entices you to partake in sin. You wrestle with yourself until your mind explodes with thoughts of jealousy and pride. God can release the chains that have you bound. Repent of your sins, and ask for forgiveness. His word delivers you from the dark into the light, creating a room destined for greatness. The dark room is only a place to hide from yourself, so open the blinds. You are God's marvelous creation—a child of the Most High King.

> **Ephesians 5:8:** "For ye were sometimes darkness, but now are ye light in the Lord: walk as children of light."

Temptation

Alcohol and drugs destroy our communities. You refuse to take part *but* smoke cigarettes instead. You say you are happy with the things that you have, *yet* you always want more to surpass your friends. You try to avoid the rumors and gossip. Now you find yourself introducing the topics. No one can say that you cheated to get by, *but* embellishing the truth is the same as a lie. You can easily say that you're not a thief or a robber, *yet* what about the office supplies you take with no bother? *Can you tell the difference between the sin and the tempter?* Remove your blinders, and take out your own splinter. Fighting temptation seems like it's hard. Your choice of free will should always lead you to God. When sin presents itself, look for an escape route. God will never leave his child without a way to get out.

> **Matthew 7:3:** "And why beholdest thou the mote that is in thy brother's eye, but considerest not the beam that is in thine own eye?"

Hard Times

Many nights are spent wondering how you will survive. You have disconnected the phone and cancelled your credit cards. What about food and how will you keep your lights on? *Sure, you could do something illegal, but what will that accomplish?* You no longer go out to eat or even to a movie. These are luxuries that you don't mind refusing. *I have a question!* Have you tried Jesus? It is the sweetest name on earth. He is a comforter, healer, and provider whenever you are in distress. *What do you have to lose?* His love is everlasting, and his mercy endures. He will never leave you lonely nor forsake you in times of trouble. So there is hope for your situation, *but* you must take the first step. Join the Believers' Club today, and wait for God to do the rest. Become a wise steward over the things that you have, and God will see that your portions last. He never gets tired of blessing you, because he is the greatest giver of all.

1 Timothy 6:17: "Charge them that are rich in this world, that they be not highminded, nor trust in uncertain riches, but in the living God, who giveth us richly all things to enjoy."

Busted

Crowded buses, long lines, and cell phones ring in a city that thrives on tourism. Store managers and supervisors rush to work waiting for consumers to spend money to meet their daily revenue. Retail merchants overprice designer bags and shoes, and food vendors are scaling back on portions. Outside a cool breeze is present as people gather to watch street performers sing and dance. The performance pleases the cheering crowd, and they pitch money into a nearby container.

A couple walking their dog stops to see what is causing all the excitement. They see the performers and burst out with laughter. Across from the performers, they hear the sound of banging drums and clashing cymbals. The couple is playfully dancing to the beat of the drums until their Rottweiler breaks loose from its chain and runs down a narrow corridor.

The 120-pound dog is charging into a line of tourists waiting to purchase tickets to a musical. The dog's muscular frame causes fear, and everyone runs into an adjacent clothing boutique. In a matter of seconds, the dog grabs a man's leg and shakes him to the ground. The couple is frantically running toward the dog shouting, *"No! No!"* The dog releases the man's leg and returns to the couple.

The couple approaches the man and apologizes for the dog's behavior, stating that the dog is usually well mannered. The man, oblivious to their remarks, tries to get up and run, until he notices one of the street performers running toward him. The street performer takes out his badge and says, "You are under arrest. You have the right to remain silent. Anything you say or do will be used against you in the court of law. You have a right to an attorney. If you do not have an attorney, one will be provided for you." As the tourists exit the boutique, the street performer tells them that he is an undercover cop. His assignment was to follow a well-known scam artist buying tickets with counterfeit money and reselling them to tourists at double the cost. The cop says to the owners, "Your dog is a hero whose brave act helped catch a wanted criminal."

What is the lesson?
God is just!

We reap what we sow! Are you sowing good or bad seeds? God wants you to refuse temptation and avoid participating in sin (Hosea 10:12). In this story, we see a couple enjoying themselves on what they thought was an ordinary day. As their dog breaks loose from its chain, we see the story shift from a mood of happiness to one of fear.

The couple, looking for a day of enjoyment, has just entered into a place of uncertainty. When the dog runs down the corridor and grabs a man's leg, we don't know at this point that the man has done anything wrong. But isn't it interesting how animals can pick up on foul behavior before we can? Just when the criminal believes he can get away with his crime, the street performer appears, disclosing that he is a police officer. You never know who is assigned to watch you for a day, so take a vow to always do good (Matthew 26:40–41).

The well-known scam artist is up to his old tricks, but this time he gets caught. Everyone has a choice to serve or reject sin. Choose the latter, because God is just, and there is always a consequence (Romans 6:23). Never feel comfortable in sin, because one night of pleasure can lead to a lifetime of imprisonment. Break the chains that have you bound, and pray for righteousness. Repent of your sins, because God's rules are not meant to be broken.

Chapter IV
"Over the Edge"

Sibling Rivalry

You were born of the same womb by a mother who loves you both. Your small hands grow too soon, and you fight with demons and ghosts. You never asked God for guidance, nor did you pray. You fell into the hands of the enemy, and now it is too late. Conflict arises, and war breaks out. *What have you done?* Blood is shed, and a child is lost. The police arrive, and your crime is exposed. The blood in your veins now turns cold. A mother is childless, *yet* she carried you both—one child to death and the other to sin. In spite of her grief, she must keep on living. *Prayer and supplication!* With the help of the Lord, she will soon forgive and pray for the child who was lost to sin. Her prayer will say, "God is righteous, and his power strengthens me from day to day."

> **Genesis 4:8–9:** "And Cain talked with Abel his brother: and it came to pass, when they were in the field, that Cain rose up against Abel his brother, and slew him. And the LORD said unto Cain, Where is Abel thy brother? And he said, I know not: Am I my brother's keeper?"

Paranoia

Trembling faces blend into the crowd. It is hard to discern who is who. Loud voices ring in your ears, but no one makes a sound. Your eyes are closed tight, and you are using only your fingers to guide you through the day. Long nights begin to weigh heavy on your mind. *What day is it?* Time stands still, and man becomes invisible in the crowd. Sorrow in your heart overwhelms you with grief. *Who has died?* Confusion sets in, while hysteria takes control. *Remain calm. Relax. This too shall pass.* Here it comes again, quickly, without warning. Your heart starts racing, and your mouth begins to foam. Look up, look up, and notice the clouds. Peace surrounds you in every direction. Conquer your fears while giving God praise. Reach up, reach up, and grab your blessings. Now, "count it all joy" (James 1:2) for the rest of your days.

> **Psalm 121:1–2, 8:** "I will lift up mine eyes unto the hills, from whence cometh my help. My help cometh from the LORD, which made heaven and earth. ... The LORD shall preserve thy going out and thy coming in from this time forth, and even for evermore."

In a Nick of Time

Confused and heartbroken, you wish that your life would end. Lonely and wounded, you welcome your self-inflicted pain. Misguided and deceived, you force a smile on a face you don't recognize. Feeling trapped and abandoned, your body is weak, so you wait for God to send you a sign. The urge to call an old friend plays around in your mind. When you pick up the phone, you forget why you dialed. Your message on the voicemail will say, "Please help me, oh Lord. I need you this day." With no time to spare, write your letter with care and prepare for your final goodbye. *Knock! Knock!* "Who is there?" you say, while slurring your words and fighting back tears from your eyes. Do you let him in, or will you pretend that you are perfectly fine? You open the door and fall on the floor. Down on bended knee, your friend says a prayer and starts to perform CPR. The urgency was heard over the phone, and he rushed to be by your side. Safe in his arms, it wasn't your time. God answered your prayer and sent you the sign. *Never alone.* God is always home, and he wants to see you survive.

Deuteronomy 30:19: "I call heaven and earth to record this day against you, that I have set before you life and death, blessing and cursing: therefore choose life, that both thou and thy seed may live."

The Collision

A bridge stretches across a busy highway that drivers travel daily. Near the top of the bridge, a serious accident has taken place. A motorcyclist was thrown from her bike and walks away from the scene with minor injuries. A man driving a white truck is unconscious, and his legs are pinned underneath the seat. In the distance, cars speed by.

Other drivers exit their cars to see if everyone involved in the accident is okay. People begin to gather around the truck to offer assistance to the truck driver.

Shortly afterward, the police and paramedics arrive at the accident scene. The paramedics transport the truck driver to the hospital hoping to save his legs, while the police officer walks over to question the motorcyclist.

The police begin to ask the woman questions about how the accident occurred. She states that she was trying to change lanes when a white truck started spiraling out of control. This caused her to lose her grip on the bike. She says that prior to the accident, her ex was driving behind her yelling and screaming. The officer asks if she could identify the type of vehicle her ex was driving, and she states that it was the blue van located on the highway.

The officer gets in his car and drives in the direction of the highway to question the person in the van. The officer approaches the van slowly and recognizes that the van is in bad condition. The rear bumper is completely gone, and the passenger-side door is smashed. The officer yells, "Are you okay?" After no response, he radios for assistance and walks behind the van. The officer looks into one of the broken windows and sees a person slumped over the steering wheel.

The policeman approaches the driver's side of the van and yells again, "Are you okay?" The woman behind the wheel speaks softly and says, "I can't move my neck." The officer, shocked to hear a women's voice, asks if she was involved in the accident that took place at the top of the bridge.

She says, "Yes, my spouse tried to cut me off, and my van rolled off the bridge onto the highway."

The officer says, "What type of vehicle was your spouse driving?"

She replies, "A white truck."

The officer looks up and sees the motorcyclist preparing to jump off the bridge. One onlooker rushes to her aid to convince her not to jump. The onlooker says that suicide is not part of God's design. God is much bigger than your situation or circumstance. As the clouds *pierce* the sky, the policeman lets out a sigh of *relief.*

What is the lesson?
God is merciful!

Only God knows the day and the hour when you will die. He doesn't need your help in making his decision. In the story, we see that a terrible accident has taken place. What and who caused the accident? We are unsure, but after talking with witnesses, we can speculate.

We see that a lady driving a motorcycle is traveling on the same bridge that her ex is traveling. We later find out that the ex happens to be female. Does this imply that the motorcyclist caused the accident? No, it simply means that when our lifestyles do not agree with God's word, then we need to re-examine ourselves. According to God's word, homosexuality is not pleasing in his sight (Genesis 19:1–11). If you are operating outside the will of God, then you are out of order.

The motorcyclist, seeing that her ex is seriously hurt in the accident, wants to commit suicide, but God has another plan for her life. God uses an onlooker to minister to her situation. God is a merciful God who will take a mess and make it a miracle (Matthew 9:20–22). Nothing is too hard for God, so don't let your trials and tribulations back you into a corner. If you ask God to remove what is not pleasing in his sight, then he will do it. All things are possible through Jesus Christ.

In the story, we also see that the ex, the woman driving the van, claims that her husband caused her to fall off the bridge onto the highway. How many times have we blamed someone else for our shortcomings? When will we take responsibility for our actions? It is not hard to repent and ask God to forgive you of your sins, but the challenge is to refuse the sin when it's presented to you (Genesis 39:2–4, 7–10).

The only person who does not speak about the accident is the one who has suffered the most—the spouse. Was he at the wrong place at the wrong time, or was God using him to show us the act of sacrifice? God has a plan for your life and wants to see it come to fruition. His love for you is so great that he gave his only begotten son, Jesus, to die for you on the cross (Matthew 1:18, 21–23). There is no greater love! So what and who caused the accident? One of the cars speeding by on the bridge.

Chapter V
"Meeting Place"

A Rose amongst Thorns

I see a flower, but the color is faded. *Is it red, pink, white, or yellow?* I smell the flower, but the scent is unknown. *Is it rosemary, jasmine, sandalwood, or lavender?* It appears to be trapped in a bushel of thorns. *Ouch!* If only I can stretch my arms a little more, I can put it in my pocket and take it home. I will place it in a vase and add warm water. I can watch it bud and then see what life has to offer. This flower infatuates me. It is a flower that looks like a rose. It is a rose amongst thorns, but still it adorns. *Ouch!* I must have it! *Did you hear that?* A voice says, "Leave it alone." I want to care for it and make it my own. I desire to touch the petals while listening to the thorns weep. *Did you hear that?* A voice says, "It was planted here for a reason, so please don't take it." No, that can't be, because I saw it first. A rose amongst so many thorns doesn't make sense. *Ouch!* I almost had it. Look at the beauty of its shape. *Did you hear that?* A voice says, "This rose is a reminder of my love. It is planted amongst thorns to show my blessings to all." I nod in agreement and then reply, "This red rose with a scent of lavender is not just for me but is a gift for all *mankind* to see."

> **Deuteronomy 28:1–2:** "And it shall come to pass, if thou shalt hearken diligently unto the voice of the LORD thy God, to observe and to do all his commandments which I command thee this day, that the LORD thy God will set thee on high above all nations of the earth: And all these blessings shall come on thee, and overtake thee, if thou shalt hearken unto the voice of the LORD thy God."

False Impressions

Tell me why you don't like others to be around you. Is it because you are afraid they might get too close, exposing your wrong habits? Or maybe you fear that they might share your secrets with anyone who will listen. What about trusting yourself to make wise choices and inviting others into your space? *Good or bad*, God has a way of revealing those secret hiding places. Stop pretending to be someone you're not, and give others a chance to get to know you. God helps you discern who your *true* friends are while disclosing to you their intentions. Look at your heart before you decide to break off *all* your connections. God places certain people in your life to help deliver your blessings.

> **Luke 8:17:** "For nothing is secret that shall not be made manifest; neither any thing hid, that shall not be known and come abroad."

Connections

Did you ever think the person you meet today is the one God has purposely sent your way? God can use anyone from the oldest to the youngest. He can use a person who lives his or her life as a good and faithful servant. If you are lonely and dismayed, then God sends a person to remind you of his grace. There are times when you must go through seasons of pain and suffering. That is when God sends a person to remind you of his love. Your situation can determine how long a person will stay. It could be for a lifetime or maybe just that day. What about the moments that a person can intimately share? God knows what you need but waits for you to ask in prayer. Thank God for sending you the person who cares the most. His name is Jesus, *a healer with just one touch.*

> **Hebrews 13:1–2:** "Let brotherly love continue. Be not forgetful to entertain strangers: for thereby some have entertained angels unawares."

Beyond Your Control

Behind an old storage shed is a black stallion that has a short and thick mane. The horse eats continually from a pile of dusty hay found across from an empty trough. The horse is expected to lead a big parade to commemorate the opening of a new factory in the town of Colorado City. The town has waited months for such an event and expects a large gathering.

The day before the parade, the owner anxiously maps out the route that his horse is expected to travel. The town mayor is offering a large sum of money to use the horse in the parade. Excited, the owner decides to go to the store to buy the horse new leather reins. When he approaches the counter, the storeowner says, "You should save your money, because the news forecasters are calling for an 80 percent chance of rain." The man replies, "This is a big event, so *surely* the parade will continue with or without rain." The man makes his purchase and then leaves the store.

While walking home, he stops to get a cup of coffee at a nearby coffee shop. He orders a small decaf with two sugars and one cream. The waitress looks at him and asks, "Do you know anyone interested in buying the three hundred pies I baked for tomorrow's event? I heard that rain is in the forecast." The man places his coffee cup on the counter and says, "This is a big event, so *surely* the parade will continue with or without rain," and leaves the shop.

The man walks up his pathway and waves to his neighbor, who is outside fixing the wheels on his wagon. His neighbor walks over and says, "Can you give me a hand with these wheels, because it looks like rain tomorrow?" The man replies, "I have a big parade to prepare for, but if you'll wait until after the parade, then I will be available." The neighbor says, "I can wait." The man retires early to bed.

Awakened out of his sleep, he hears a loud screeching noise from behind the shed. He goes outside to find the horse lying on its side, wailing in pain. The man knocks frantically on his neighbor's door to ask for a ride to the veterinary hospital. The neighbor replies, "My wagon is not fixed. Remember, you said that if I waited until after the parade, then you would help." So the man walks into town looking for a doctor to examine the horse. After searching for twenty minutes, he finds a doctor who agrees to see the horse but demands his payment up front. The man recalls the leather reigns he bought earlier and offers them to the doctor as a form of payment.

When they return to the house, the horse is found lying on its back with a void expression in its eyes. The doctor pronounces the horse dead from food poisoning and notifies the newspapers the next morning. The man is heartbroken about his horse dying and that the parade was canceled due to rain. Sadly, the man invites friends over to say their goodbyes to the horse. The first guest to arrive is the waitress from the coffee shop, carrying a box of pies.

What is the lesson?
God is omnipotent!

We often wonder about that inner voice that tells us to go right or left. God gives us clear instructions when we seek his presence. In this story, we see that a big parade is to take place in Colorado City. A prominent horse is selected to lead the parade, when a tragedy hits.

Throughout the story, the owner of the horse is impatient and neglects the warning signs. Oftentimes we have our own agenda in life instead of operating in God's plan. When we put our own needs before God's, we risk falling into temptation. The owner became proud and let greed dictate his every move (Matthew 26:14–16). God will always find a way to humble us so that we don't get too big headed.

In the story, we see that the storeowner, the waitress, and the neighbor state that rain will cancel the parade. But notice in the story how the events play out. The horse has been eating from a pile of tainted hay, indicating that something is about to happen. The owner is persistent that the parade will continue regardless of rain. How many times have we said, "It's my way or no way"? God controls every situation, even the rain (Leviticus 26:4).

When the horse dies, the owner is left to find help on his own. Some circumstances in life we make difficult because of our disobedience to God (Psalm 7:15–16). Receiving God's word for our lives can eliminate embarrassment down the road. This is shown when the waitress arrives at the house with the pies. Imagine how you would feel knowing that you could have heeded the warning signs instead of waiting until the Last Call!

Chapter VI
"No Limits"

Final Destination

Everyone's path in life is different. No two are the *exact* same. Our paths may cross from time to time, but *eventually* we go separate ways. Certain aspects of my journey may be similar to yours, causing the *same* hurt and pain. My journey may last as long as yours, but in time the seasons change. Your journey may lead you to a new beginning that requires a fast pace. You may start out on a crooked path but end on one that's straight. God orders your steps, so if you fall, just get back up. Your journey is not over; there is more to be done. If you are looking for compassion, you may not receive it. Stop looking, and pick up the tools that you need: *a God-fearing spirit and a desire to succeed.*

> **Isaiah 42:16:** "And I will bring the blind by a way that they knew not; I will lead them in paths that they have not known: I will make darkness light before them, and crooked things straight. These things will I do unto them, and not forsake them."

Closer to God than the Day Before

I stand before a crowd, and my prayer resonates with power. I hear the master speak to deliver souls from sin. I am given my assignment to preach the Good News! Christ redeems us all if we repent and believe. Believe that Jesus died for us so that we might be saved. Confess with your mouth that Jesus is Lord. Believe in your heart that he was raised from the dead. Then salvation is yours, sealed to redemption. Everyone can see the change and the anointing that takes place. The Holy Spirit has arrived, and the blessings shall go forth. *Unsaved households, broken marriages, and famine lands—restored.* I bring my sermon to a close and bless his holy name. I thank God for his grace that kept me through the day. Praise and worship for me will never be the same. I have seen God's glory and heard him call my name.

> **Luke 4:18–19:** "The Spirit of the Lord is upon me, because he hath anointed me to preach the gospel to the poor; he hath sent me to heal the brokenhearted, to preach deliverance to the captives, and recovering of sight to the blind, to set at liberty them that are bruised. To preach the acceptable year of the Lord."

Lighthouse

Closer! Closer! Use God's light to guide you to the lighthouse. I see you starting to go adrift. *Don't be afraid!* Just keep steering. God can protect you against the raging waters. I know it's getting dark out there, but you can make it. Listen to God's voice. He creates visibility for you. *Do you believe?* The light directs you to your destination. God created the storm to help strengthen your faith. The light is your reference, so watch for it with diligence. *It's not hidden!* See how it moves in a circular motion, shining for everyone to see. Glorify God as he brings you out of the deepest part of the sea. *Starting to waver!* Steady yourself on the ship, and wait for the miracle. The sky opens up with a powerful voice, causing the wind to stop and the waves to cease! The lighthouse is awaiting your expected arrival. *Is your light on?*

> **Psalm 27:1:** "The LORD is my light and my salvation; whom shall I fear? the LORD is the strength of my life; of whom shall I be afraid?"

Boat Ride

It has been a long week for Burt, a postman who works at a busy post office in downtown Manhattan. Today, Burt decides to go to the Eastern Shore in Maryland for a boat ride. The scenery always relaxes him and reminds him of the time his family gathered at the park to celebrate his sixteenth birthday. Today he notices that the water is rising higher than usual. He believes that by sundown the water will settle to a calmer state.

Burt slowly lowers himself into the nine-foot rowboat and uses his left foot to push away from the dock. He positions himself in the center of the boat and uses wooden oars to steer himself northeast of the mainland. After rowing for about fifteen minutes, he can hear the water crashing against the boat in all directions. The strong waves cause him to lose his balance. As he quickly moves his oars, he recalls the early days of his childhood.

At age six, Burt pretended to be a famous orator. In his baritone voice, he dreamed of delivering speeches in front of the White House. He stood with his back straight and arms to his side while rehearsing lines in the mirror. He recalls thinking how life was so easy, with fewer responsibilities and no worries, at age thirteen. Many nights were spent watching television and reading horror books. He was never scared of anything. He was always the strong one in the family.

He remembers going to college to study graphic design at age eighteen. His dream of drawing a wall mural to express the various plights of Americans was always a desire of his. Burt recalls dropping out of college and stealing his first car at age twenty. Although he didn't serve time in prison, the mere thought of his deeds makes him queasy inside. Now at age forty, he has two kids and believes that life has nothing more to offer him.

Burt wants another chance to see his kids. He wants the opportunity to tell them how much he loves them. His worst fear is that he may never get that chance again. Burt panics and breaks one of the oars. He uses his right hand to help guide the boat when it hits a large wave. He falls into the cold water, grimacing from the pain. Unable to relocate the boat, he is forced to swim toward the shoreline.

Burt swims in the water for nearly an hour, when he hears a voice that says, "Don't give up." Although his arms and legs are tired, he looks around for help. Burt notices a tree and grabs the top of the tree branch. As the hard water hits his backside, his grip loosens, and he falls. *Stay focused!* With an unrelenting zeal in his eyes, Burt swims closer to the branch and grabs hold tightly. His faith strengthens, and he makes it to shore. Shivering and cold, Burt gazes at the sky and thinks of his mother's last words, "Life is what you make it, so live each day as if it is your last, because tomorrow is not promised."

What is the lesson?
God is faithful!

Do you know where you are headed in life? Have you prayed to God to direct your paths and lead you to your destiny? In the story, we see that Burt, a local postman, has become dissatisfied with his life. He believes that his life is monotonous and decides to go for a boat ride. Although he positions himself in the center of the boat, he wavers when the wave hits.

How many times have you set out to do a specific task and failed to follow through? Are you still on a mission for God, or have you taken a detour? God will never lead you astray, so it is important to appreciate what he has given you (Jeremiah 29:11). In the story, Burt recalls various times in his life when he was happy and in control. Now he is fighting for his life—a life that he is not sure is worth saving.

Burt thinks about his children and begins to feel sorry for himself. This is shown when he panics and breaks one of the oars. He struggles to find his balance and falls into the water. Burt does not realize that the water is symbolic of God's word, so he is in the right place to receive his deliverance (Mark 4:37–39). Burt hears the voice of God saying, "Don't give up." Sometimes all we need is a little encouragement to keep us going.

I encourage you today to hold on, because your living is not in vain. God is faithful, and he will provide for your every need. You must stop complaining about your situation and start praising God for what he has done in your life. When the tide comes in, remember to remain calm and wait for God to show up. He is an "on time" God who will steer you on the path to righteousness.

Chapter VII
"Born Identity"

What's in a Name?

Your name has value and is worth more than you know. Your name travels with you wherever you go. Your name is your character and speaks volumes to a crowd. Your name says that you are trustworthy and honest. Your name tells a story of how your life began. Your name is a picture of what you *will* become. Your name is royalty that leaves behind a legacy of kings and queens. *Now* think about the name Jesus and how he gave his life for you and me. Jesus is a name that saved the world and suffered at Calvary. It is a name that heals the sick and gives sight to the blind. *Jesus! Jesus!* It is a name that is sweeter than any name around. Jesus holds the names in the Lamb's book of life.

Sign here X_____.

Is your name written in the book?

> **Proverbs 22:1:** "A GOOD name is rather to be chosen than great riches, and loving favour rather than silver and gold."

Reflections

Take a look in the mirror. *Don't move!* Tell me what you see. Are your eyes too small and your nose too wide? Are your lips too thin and your ears too large? Do you like your hips, and what about your thighs? Look again; you might be surprised. God has created you in his image. You are wonderfully made. Don't let anyone tell you different. God created the sun, moon, and stars. What makes you think he doesn't know who you are? He has numbered the "very hairs of your head" (Luke 12:7), and knows what you are thinking before it is said. You are his child, and he loves you unconditionally. He gave his only begotten son to die for your sins and grief. Stretch out your arms and tilt your head to the right. This is how he died for you on the cross that night. So turn around slowly. What image do you see? *A reflection of the beauty that lives in you and me.*

> **Genesis 1:26:** "And God said, Let us make man in our image, after our likeness: and let them have dominion over the fish of the sea, and over the fowl of the air, and over the cattle, and over all the earth, and over every creeping thing that creepeth upon the earth."

A Powerful Testimony

Did you know that hiding your pain enlarges the wound? Ignoring your past gives you a false sense of identity. Embrace who you are, and acknowledge God's plan for your life. His plan is to deliver you from bondage and use your story to bless someone else. Don't be embarrassed by the things you have overcome. "For the battle is not yours," but it is only God's fight to win (2 Chr. 20:15). Boldly confront your demons, and confess each one of your sins. Then watch God show up to defeat your enemies. As you talk about your trials, *always* flash a smile. God gives you the strength and makes it all worthwhile. People *might* judge you based on what they see. Don't let *that* deter you from upholding your beliefs. You never know—something said or done might make them confess and give their lives to Christ. *Who wouldn't want that?*

> **Psalm 19:7:** "The law of the LORD is perfect, converting the soul: the testimony of the LORD is sure, making wise the simple."

In the Heat of the Day

One hot summer day, a car speeds past a man hitchhiking in the middle of the road. The man chases behind the car, yelling at the driver to stop, but the car keeps going. The man is tired, and the heat blurs his vision. As he walks along the road, he thinks about his family and career. It was only yesterday that he was traveling to Phoenix to attend a conference when his car broke down.

He wanted to impress the board members, so he chose to wear his best suit and tie. His belt and watch were the last items he put on before leaving the house. Although he was concerned about the heat in Phoenix, he decided not to have the car serviced. The car was two years old and had never given him any problems.

The sun is beaming down on his face, and he can barely keep his eyes open. He reaches up to wipe off the perspiration and notices blood on his hands. Without a mirror to tell where the blood is coming from, he uses his belt buckle to see his reflection. All he can make out is that his nose looks smaller and his eyes appear swollen. *Could he have been bitten by some type of insect?*

The man begins to yell out for help, when he remembers that he has a white handkerchief in his left back pocket. He pulls out the handkerchief and starts to cough. His mind drifts back to the meeting he had with his boss a few days ago. The boss told him to make sure his presentation delivered a bonus-signing offer. He worked all weekend preparing his proposal, trying to get the board members' approval. He even missed church, thinking that God knows his heart. *Does anyone recognize that he is five hours past his scheduled time to present?*

The man stops by a bush to rest his legs and begins to remove his watch. He looks at the watch, but the numbers are unclear. The leather band is ripping apart and burns his arm profusely. He remembers his wife giving him the watch on their anniversary. The thought of carrying it becomes unbearable. The extra weight brings tears to his eyes, and he throws it down on the ground.

He removes his badly torn shirt and wraps it around his head. He gets up and starts running with all his might. He trips on a stone lying in the middle of the road. Face down in the dirt, the man turns the stone over and reads, "*To live, you must die.*"

What is the lesson?
God is sovereign!

How do you balance family and career? If God is not the center of your life, then it is difficult. In the story, we see that the man is consumed with work. He spends most of his time preparing presentations and attending business trips. He has chosen his work over the church. God wants us to attend church so we can fellowship with other believers in Christ (Hebrews 10:25).

It is time to build a relationship with God. God wakes you up in morning so that you are productive on your job. God covers your family when you are away. Stop and think about his grace and mercy. We see that the man is five hours past his time to present. The number five symbolizes grace.

On his journey, the man begins bleeding, and we see his vulnerability. The blood is symbolic of cleansing and purification (1 John 1:7). It is a transformation that takes place when the man does not recognize his reflection in his belt buckle. The man is in pain and remembers the handkerchief in his back pocket. Here the cloth symbolizes his desire for healing (Acts 19:12).

The man is tired and takes time to rest by a bush. The watch given to him by his wife is too heavy, so he removes it. Are you carrying around extra weight that is stopping your spiritual growth? God wants to be the focus of our lives, and that means he must come before our spouses and children.

In the story, we see that the man trips over a stone that reads, "To live, you must die." This statement simply says that we ought to deny our flesh every day in order to become more like Christ (Matthew 16:24–26). God governs our lives, and he alone reigns supreme.

Chapter VIII
"Problem Solved"

The Ultimatum

Mistakes are often made, *yet* we are able to forgive one another. Prescription drugs invade our cabinets, *yet* we choose not to overdose. Violent crimes are committed daily, *yet* we remain model citizens. Gangs take over our neighborhoods, *yet* we still have hope for a better tomorrow. Have you passed your test today? Or did you sleep in? We can change our attitude, our response to trials, and our mindset. Can you imagine a world where we do our part and everyone does his or her part? I hear you saying, "That would be nice if we lived in an ideal world." So how do we solve this dilemma called life? The answer is simple: *give*. Giving is a vital key to your happiness and joy. When you obey God's commandments and pay your tithes, you reap the benefits of the harvest. You can also give your time or generous words to help another brother/sister going through a hard situation. Wake up every morning and ask yourself, "Who can I help today?" You know the famous line, "Am I my brother's keeper?"(Gen. 4:9). And your answer is?

> **Luke 6:38:** "Give, and it shall be given unto you; good measure, pressed down, and shaken together, and running over, shall men give into your bosom. For with the same measure that ye mete withal it shall be measured to you again."

Patchwork

Pieces of your soul are patched together to make a quilt. Memories of your life are on display for everyone to see. *Upper-right corner.* Are you laughing or crying? *Lower- left corner.* Are you grieving or at peace? Is there a patch for righteousness and one for forgiveness? How will you fill in the missing pieces? Let's start with a patch centered on your religious beliefs. God is the creator of all things, and his greatness is beyond measure. He is a loving and merciful God who advocates obedience. He blesses you with finances and supplies your every need. If given another chance, what would you do differently? You can break generational curses if you let God intercede. God is all-knowing and all-powerful, a wonderful friend indeed. *What does your quilt say about you?*

> **James 1:25:** "But whoso looketh into the perfect law of liberty, and continueth therein, he being not a forgetful hearer, but a doer of the work, this man shall be blessed in his deed."

Surviving the Test

Tested and tried. Beaten and bruised. I watch my body fail and my mind go astray. I reached my breaking point and wanted to give in, *yet* I thought of how God has kept me and promised to heal my infirmities. I thought of how he died for my sins and bled on the cross to save me. Think of how Jesus was besieged and humiliated in front of a hostile crowd. Our Jesus suffered *yet* prayed for those who made a mockery of him. *What courage, what obedience, and what love!* My pain can never add up to the suffering that Jesus endured. My problems can never outweigh the many miracles that Jesus performed. Neither sickness nor death can make me deny my God, the Savior of my soul. I was put in the furnace to strengthen my faith, so I learned to trust God with each passing day. I am *still* here, delivered from the fire—cleaned, refined, and unscathed.

> **Romans 8:35–39:** "Who shall separate us from the love of Christ? shall tribulation, or distress, or persecution, or famine, or nakedness, or peril, or sword? As it is written, For thy sake we are killed all the day long; we are accounted as sheep for the slaughter. Nay, in all these things we are more than conquerors through him that loved us. For I am persuaded, that neither death, nor life, nor angels, nor principalities, nor powers, nor things present, nor things to come, Nor height, nor depth, nor any other creature, shall be able to separate us from the love of God, which is in Christ Jesus our Lord."

A Season of Winter

The cold and bitter wind whips through you, stinging your arms and legs. Your fingertips are frozen, and your lips are bruised from winter's beatings. The line is long as you wait for the doors of the soup kitchen to open. You turn around to look at the clock placed on the outside of the old Christian building. *One hour to go.* You count to see how many people are standing in front of you. *Seventy-five people.* The missionaries stop serving at one hundred people.

With barely a sweater to keep you warm and no hat, you notice snow lightly falling on the ground. *Can it get any worse?* You have not eaten a complete meal in four days and desire to have turkey, stuffing, yams, and green beans. In your heart, you know that you will settle for whatever the missionaries will offer. You will even eat the leftover portions from their kitchen tables. *Forty-five minutes to go.*

With the snow falling heavier now, you envision yourself in front of a fireplace surrounded by family and friends. Your siblings won't speak to you because of a decision you made years ago to sell the family house after your parents passed. You tried to notify them by telephone and mail, but you were unable to reach them. You decided to spend the money on a business venture. You told yourself you were investing in your future. Your partner walked away with all the profits, leaving you homeless.

Thirty minutes to go. Life on the streets is hard, but you have managed to stay out of trouble. You are hopeful that your situation will get better. For the past three years, you have been eating meals at homeless shelters and hanging around restaurants. No one wants to hire someone without a residence.

No longer able to feel your hands or your feet, you pray to God that death does not consume you this way. You always wanted to die peacefully in your sleep, not from hypothermia. You look around and notice that the line has extended down the street past the bakery. You try to blow warm air into your hands, but the mere thought makes you nauseated. *Fifteen minutes to go.*

Waiting for another fifteen minutes seems like an eternity. You feel sorry for those who won't make it into the shelter. Maybe you will save something for them to eat when you are done. As you rock back and forth to warm up, you feel someone nudging you from behind.

"Can I help you?" you say.

The man slowly looks up at you and says, "I am starving. Do you mind if I get in front of you?"

You immediately move behind the man, allowing him to reposition himself in front of you. You smile at the thought of helping someone along the way during this rough time.

Commotion breaks out, and people are yelling at you for letting the man cut in line. To avoid further problems, you agree to move to the back of the line, allowing the man to take your spot. Everyone agrees, and you are relieved that the man gets a chance to eat.

The doors to the soup kitchen swing open, and everyone starts pushing and shoving. You try to remain calm, hoping that you don't lose your place in the line. One of the missionaries stops the line in front of you and says, "Sorry, you are one hundred and one. This facility is no longer serving people." The line begins to disperse when another missionary runs out to announce that a newer facility has just opened two blocks away and will serve the remaining people.

Ten minutes later, you are enjoying a hot meal in a newer facility when someone approaches you about a job and offers you a place to stay. The gratitude you feel goes beyond words. You say thank you and smile at the thought of having a fresh start in life.

What is the lesson?
God is love!

Have you extended loving kindness to a brother, sister, or neighbor? God requires us to love one another just as he loves us (Ephesians 5:2). In the story, we see a person waiting outside in inclement weather for the doors of a soup kitchen to open. The reader is allowed a glimpse into the character's life as he/she demonstrates a selfless act of love (1 Corinthians. 13:3–4).

In the story, there are seventy-five people standing in front of the main character waiting to be fed. Knowing that the missionaries will stop serving at a hundred people, we understand the urgency for the countdown. What we begin to see is that despite the negative conditions, the main character remains hopeful and optimistic. There are times in our life when we are faced with difficult situations. Do we fall apart, or can we say that God is still good (Job 23:10–12)?

In the story, the character loses a home, job, and family. The character is forced to live on the street, but does not resort to violence. In fact, the character takes a moment to think about others in a time of despair. The character is willing to give up his/her space in line and risks losing a meal to help someone in need (Romans 15:1–2). We have seen this act of kindness before when Jesus feeds the multitude with five loaves of bread and two fishes (Matthew 14:16–20).

How many of us are willing to give our last? Are you willing to put others' needs before your own? From the story, we know that everyone in line is hungry, but we see that someone is bold enough to ask permission to cut in line. What are you asking God for today? Are you sincere in your asking, or do you simply want a handout?

God can change your life around and bless you in the presence of your enemies (Psalm 23:5–6). You must be willing to sacrifice and let go of some selfish ways. When we step out on faith, only good things can happen. In the story, the main character enjoys a meal at one of the newer facilities, accepts a job offer, and finds a place to stay. God will deliver you from winter's beatings and fill your heart with warmth. Your reward in showing love is to know that what God has done for others he can do for you.

Chapter IX
"The Big Picture"

Position for Hire

Let God use you to carry out his mission—*a mission to save souls and to bless individuals*. Based on your credentials, you are the best candidate for the position. God has checked out your references and stamped the resume, "Approved." Now you must complete what God has called you to do. Are you afraid that you will fail at your assigned task? He has scheduled you for training and prepared you for the test. There is no pass or fail, only a simple *yes!* Say yes to the Father, the Son, and the Holy Ghost—for these three are one leading you to your purpose. God gives you the wisdom and the knowledge to succeed. This position was intended for only you to receive. He has given you the confidence to recruit other workers. The word of God *must* be used as your referral. The reward you receive is better than a paycheck. It is God's gift to the world—eternal life through Jesus Christ.

> **Matthew 28:18–20:** "And Jesus came and spake unto them, saying, All power is given unto me in heaven and in earth. Go ye therefore, and teach all nations, baptizing them in the name of the Father, and of the Son, and of the Holy Ghost: Teaching them to observe all things whatsoever I have commanded you: and, lo, I am with you alway, even unto the end of the world."

Active Duty

You thought you could handle a position so high. You are watching others in ministry where everyone is complaining. *Did you make the right decision?* You attend leaders' meetings and choir rehearsals. God gave you the gifts, so use it to his glory. As a believer in Christ, you can grow and make a difference. *Take it one day at a time.* Sow your seed, and serve him with gladness. God provides you with the armor needed for the battle. He helps you to get along with the other believers in Christ. Enlist with the rest of the soldiers who are called for active duty. Position yourself in his holy tabernacle, and worship God with his troops. The purpose is to lead others to Christ and to show them that God lives in you. *Calling all soldiers!*

> **1 Corinthians 12:7:** "But the manifestation of the Spirit is given to every man to profit withal."

Time Management

At times you think the work you do goes unnoticed. You schedule meetings and answer phones, *yet* you stay focused. No time for rest. There is too much to do in a twenty-four-hour day. There is no one to help, but you *always* make time to pray. Rest assured that God hears and knows your every word. He is smiling down on his child while showering you with love. God knows the tasks that lie ahead but *never* overwhelms you. Stay in the word, and believe that God will give you comfort. The work you do for the Lord is *always* recognized. Remain steadfast, stay strong, and know that God is on your side.

> **1 Corinthians 15:58:** "Therefore, my beloved brethren, be ye stedfast, unmoveable, always abounding in the work of the Lord, forasmuch as ye know that your labour is not in vain in the Lord."

Call to Action

The concrete walls move closer, pushing old furniture out of the way. The ceiling drops, crushing the smallest item into pieces. The smell of dampness and mold is surrounding the entire area. The sound of loud bricks smashed against the pavement is heard from blocks away.

The bulldozer charges into the building, determined to leave nothing behind. There are no memories to ponder upon and no one to recall the happy times. *Is this necessary?* Is there no other way to renovate, refurbish, or even preserve the seventy-year-old building that resembles a pile of ashes? What will the children think when they ride their bikes or the pedestrians as they jog to the next block for better scenery?

I can scarcely make out the once-vibrant red color that grabbed my attention from across the street. As I look at the building, my heart starts racing, and my hands become numb. I can taste the dryness in my mouth as I walk toward the pile of ashes. To my surprise, I can still hear laughter coming from the cafeteria. "Don't forget to cut the lights off when you leave," was Rita's favorite statement before leaving work each day. It doesn't matter if the lights are on or off *this* day. No one cares enough to stop the politicians from destroying a historic building that contained life.

Many people are without jobs. *Is this necessary?* Who will listen to the cries of those that can no longer afford housing or to buy food from their local market? Has health care become so expensive that our children can't go to the doctor's office or even the dentist for a check-up? Someone must have the answers, or maybe it can be found in *this* pile of ashes.

I jump over the four-foot fence and bend down to scoop up a cupful of dirt and twigs. I slowly bring the pile to my nose when the smell of burnt coal shoots through my nostrils. I begin to cough uncontrollably and return the ashes back to their former state. *Something is not right.* When did we become complacent that nothing matters anymore?

As I turn to leave, my foot becomes entangled in what appears to be a vine. This is the only form of life that exists among the ruins. With a sigh of relief, I leave the deserted site. From across the street, I watch the remaining pieces of fallen debris overcome the plant. With no place to hide, the plant, along with the memories of the old historic building, ceases to exist. As my feelings of sadness fade, I decide to never let this happen again without a fight.

What is the lesson?
God is courage!

Can you make a difference in your community, church, or home? God wants to use you to change a negative situation into a positive one. In the story, the character is upset about a decision to raze a seventy-year-old building. This is a building where many people have worked and shared in special times. Members of the community could have come together to voice their concerns during home association meetings or during neighborhood rallies. God gives us the courage to step out in faith (Deuteronomy 31:6).

In the story, the character suggests refurbishing the old building. Sometimes in life we try to fix up our problems rather than turn to God for a solution. Let's keep in mind that once we get saved, we must ask God to remove those things that hinder our progress, even if that means removing familiar places and friends (Psalm 139:23–24).

In the story, the character reflects on the last moments spent in the building. The person picks up a pile of dirt and twigs hoping to smell a sweet aroma but instead smells burnt coal. God formed man from the dust of the ground, so that means we are dirt (Genesis 2:7). We can choose to live a life devoted to God with a sweet smell of spices or live a life that is offensive and stinks of death.

God wants to take us to the next level in our spiritual walk. He wants us to exercise faith and courage in obeying his commandments. God has a purpose for our lives, so get involved. Let's be proactive instead of inactive.

Chapter X
"No Doubt"

Nature Walk

Take my hand and walk with me through the land of promise. *Not too fast*! I want to take time to enjoy the scenery and to smell the flowers. Join me as I sing a song of how I have overcome sorrow. I am singing praises to my God yesterday, today, and tomorrow. My soul is overwhelmed with joy, unspeakable joy. Look at how tall the trees stand. They watch as God pours out blessings on his devoted lambs. Let's not forget the birds that fly in the vast blue sky. They take flight *higher and higher*. I marvel at God's wonderful design. Butterflies are embellished with vibrant colors and ladybugs gather to display their spots. Families of deer rejoice on a land that is rich. A profound site—*a trail of God's splendor that peacefully connects the heart, soul, and mind.*

> **2 Peter 1:4:** "Whereby are given unto us exceeding great and precious promises: that by these ye might be partakers of the divine nature, having escaped the corruption that is in the world through lust."

Falling Snow

Snow from heaven is sent your way to fulfill God's word. *Are you watching?* Pure snow is sent that waters the earth and refreshes the soul. You get a tranquil feeling when the snow touches your face. Delicate snow resembles a smile and captures your heart. It is a picture so lovely that the ground blushes from the sight. Soft snow vanishes in your hand and leaves you amazed. *It is beauty in its natural state.* White snow is sure to brighten even the darkest of days. There is no evidence of pain and no reminder of sorrow. Pieces large and small occupy a space filled with hope and promise. It *is* falling snow used to show one of God's most evident signs.

> **Isaiah 55:10–11:** "For as the rain cometh down, and the snow from heaven, and returneth not thither, but watereth the earth, and maketh it bring forth and bud, that it may give seed to the sower, and bread to the eater: So shall my word be that goeth forth out of my mouth: it shall not return unto me void, but it shall accomplish that which I please, and it shall prosper in the thing whereto I sent it."

Sunset

Look at the sunset and see how the sky illuminates with a soft aura of orange and blues. Projected rays that mark their territory flourish outward. *Behold*! It is a sight that reminds me of a mother embracing her newborn child—a moment in time captured on film that releases joy and happiness. *Downward*! The sun, so bright, waves goodbye to those passing by. Hidden in the clouds, I *still* see an outline of its remaining beauty. It is an image I hold dear and recall to memory when the world is in dismay. A sunset lights up the earth and warms my heart. A sunset praises God, along with the moon and the stars.

> **Psalm 148:1–4:** "Praise ye the LORD. Praise ye the LORD from the heavens: praise him in the heights. Praise ye him, all his angels: praise ye him, all his hosts. Praise ye him, sun and moon: praise him, all ye stars of light. Praise him, ye heavens of heavens, and ye waters that be above the heavens."

Epiphany

As the sun begins to set, a fisherman pulls his boat up to the dock. The fisherman notices that his fishing rod is bent and decides to fix it. He uses some pliers and a hammer to reposition the rod back into shape. Satisfied that the rod is fixed, he gets off the boat and heads home. While staggering up the steps, he looks back and observes two rays of light. The man places the fishing rod on the steps and walks toward the boat.

He boards the boat and hears a loud noise coming from the lower deck. He looks around and grabs an empty beer bottle to use as a weapon. Once he enters the lower deck, he spots a small cat running across his feet. He follows the cat to the upper part of the deck and looks into the sky. The fisherman realizes that a storm is approaching and decides to return home. Satisfied that the rays of light were from the storm, he discards the bottle.

The wind picks up, and thunder is soon heard. As he walks up the steps, he notices his fishing rod is gone. The angry fisherman surveys the entire house but sees no one. He enters the house where the *same* cat that was on the boat walks across his path. He follows the cat upstairs and finds the fishing rod lying on the floor next to the bedroom window. He looks out the window, toward the boat, and becomes paralyzed for two minutes. The boat begins to submerge into the water until it is no longer visible. The fisherman picks up his fishing rod and notices that the rod is *still* bent. He looks toward the hallway and watches the cat slowly disappear.

What is the lesson?
God is truth!

Are you a casual drinker or smoker? Are you a person who is easily angered or annoyed? In the story, we see that a fisherman leaves his boat after fixing a broken fishing rod. He returns back to the boat after noticing flashing lights. Once on the boat, he looks for a weapon and picks up an empty beer bottle. *Stop*! God wants us to present our bodies as a living sacrifice to him—free from harmful substances (Romans 12:1–2). What are you putting into your body? You are required to be sober, watchful, and of good behavior, waiting on the Lord (1 Peter 4:7).

The story then tells us that the fisherman sees a cat run across his path. The cat is symbolic of the fisherman's perceptive insight. It leads him to the upper deck, where he looks into the sky and notices a storm coming. How often do we follow our gut instinct? Do you ever say, "Something told me not to do that," but you do it anyway?

After returning home, the fisherman's rod disappears. He becomes angry and surveys the home. Oftentimes, we tend to let our emotions control the way we handle life situations. Anger breeds trouble. If you are annoyed by certain events, then take a minute to cool off (Psalm 37:7–8). Retaliating and fighting is not the way to solve a problem—prayer is.

Later in the story, we see that the cat appears again. This time the cat leads the fisherman upstairs to the fishing rod. Sometimes it is hard for us to notice our character flaws until our litter is exposed. We can go through life thinking we can do no wrong until that one day of awakening (1 Peter 1:18-25). In the story, the man looks out the window to see his boat submerged under water. His livelihood is immediately taken from him. Let's always give God praise for the things that we have; otherwise, we become ungrateful.

The bent fishing rod represents God's ability to reject our unclean offerings (Amos 5:22–24). If you are not living according to scripture, then you are living a lie. Release the things that God wants to remove from your life today, because God's word is truth.

Chapter XI
"Service Check"

Authentic Praise

Your walk with Christ is tested each day, so always give God authentic praise. Your praise and worship must come from your heart. Be led in God's presence without any doubts. Live a life that is pleasing to the Most High. His grace and mercy will always reside. The gift of salvation is given to you. Walk in assurance that God's word is the truth. Enter the sanctuary expecting a change. God will show up with a word for that day. The word you receive *must* minister to your life. Others should see the power of Christ. The power that strengthens you from day to day is the *same* power that requires authentic praise.

> **Philippians 4:8:** "Finally, brethren, whatsoever things are true, whatsoever things are honest, whatsoever things are just, whatsoever things are pure, whatsoever things are lovely, whatsoever things are of good report; if there be any virtue, and if there be any praise, think on these things."

Sweet Dreams

God is your refuge when nothing seems clear. Seek him in the morning before your day begins. Open your Bible and read God's holy word. Pray and ask for guidance before you go to work. Greet everyone you meet with a cheerful smile. It only takes a second to be cordial and nice. Ask God to use you to help someone in need, and then show yourself friendly to those who mistreat you. Serve everyone with gladness and joy. God will pour out a blessing that there's no room to store. Learn to repent for each one of your sins, even the ones that you thought of committing. At the end of the day, when you lay down to rest, remember to thank God for keeping you safe. As you drift into a peaceful sleep, envision yourself standing on God's holy ground. Now reverence the Lord and receive your crown.

Proverbs 3:24: "When thou liest down, thou shall not be afraid: yea, thou shalt lie down, and thou sleep shall be sweet."

Intervention

Avail yourself to God, and he will intervene on your behalf. No problem is too great or small for God to handle. Lend an ear, and listen to his voice. The voice tells you to walk by faith, not by sight, to exercise patience in well doing, and to extend brotherly kindness to all those in need. God delivers you from bondage and diseases. *Are you ready for your miracle?* Your blessings will be far more than you can imagine. Start a new chapter in your life, and let God tell the story of how he brought you out of despair. The power of healing begins with your submission to do God's will. *Are you ready for your miracle?*

Romans 8:26: "Likewise the Spirit also helpeth our infirmities: for we know not what we should pray for as we ought: but the Spirit itself maketh intercession for us with groanings which cannot be uttered."

Someone Is Watching

Do you see me walking down the street with my head held high and my face gleaming with expectation? I can tell the world is in dismay because I hear the fire engines and the police officers rush past my swift-moving feet. Before I cross the street, I take time to check my surroundings. *Right, left!* I see the other pedestrians rushing to make their 8:30 start time and to make that first cup of morning coffee. As I enter the tall building that sits on the corner of Washington and Broadway, I check my watch: 8:20 a.m.

I have time to pick up a copy of the *USA Today* and read a few headlines while waiting for the elevator. I work on the tenth floor, which makes it difficult to leave work on time. I usually take the stairs to avoid the conflict of pushing and shoving on the elevators. *Ding!* Here we go. My day usually starts with a few hellos and pleasantries like, "How are you doing?" When I walk into my office, I see everyone either working on their laptops or talking to their neighbors. I speak in my usual perky voice, "Good morning!"

For the past four weeks, interns have invaded our office with questions about financial billing statements and revenue costs. I suppose they are training to take my position as assistant director of marketing, but I have no evidence to support my notions. I continue my route to my desk when I hear the sound of someone clearing her throat. I turn around to observe a short, stout woman with curly hair smiling at me.

"Hi. How are you? My name is Christy," she says.

I look at this person, who appears to be much older than twenty years of age, and say, "Hi, my name is Rebecca, and I have been assigned to mentor you this week. Welcome to Thomas and Thomas Associates."

I was hoping to enjoy a few minutes alone in my office before badgering Christy with the use of our financial acronyms. However, Christy seems eager to start work. She refuses to let me check my phone messages or even to close my office window that someone has opened. I walk around the office introducing Christy to my entire staff and even help her unpack the office supplies that are waiting for her on her desk. I excuse myself and tell her that I will be right back. I almost knock over the guard standing outside my office trying to make a fast escape.

"Hi, Ms. Rebecca," the guard says.

"Oh, hi, Jimmy. I am in a rush and need to return a few phone calls before the intern starts questioning me for today. Can I help you with anything?" I say.

"No," he replies. "I just noticed that your window was open and decided to close it for you. I hope I didn't disturb you too much."

"You could never disturb me. Thanks for closing the window," I say. I tell Jimmy the window was open prior to my arrival. He says he will look into it for me.

In about ten minutes, Christy is going to be knocking at my door expecting me to share all I know about finances, but first I must return Mike's call. Mike is the director of promotion and sales, and he wants to meet with me during lunch to discuss a few clients. *Knock, Knock!*

"Please come in," I say. "Hey, Christy, I didn't forget about you. I was just about to make a phone call."

Christy looks at me nervously and says, "Ms. Rebecca, do you mind if I have a word with you?"

I reply, "Go ahead, you can ask me anything."

She says that she wants to discuss her salary. She was told that her starting salary would be twenty thousand dollars, but after talking with some of the other interns, she found out that her starting salary is fifteen thousand dollars. I tell her to refer the matter to human resources and not to me. She walks out of my office furious. I sadly remember those days when a paycheck was my main concern.

Mike is expecting to meet me in an hour at Rockford's Deli. *Knock, Knock!* "Come in," I say. It is Samantha, the receptionist at the front desk. She says that there is a package for me that requires my signature. I thank her and go out front to sign for the delivery. I return to my office to find my papers on the floor from the cold breeze blowing through the window. *Is someone playing games with me?* I look out the window to see if I can spot anyone from below. Surprisingly, I can see directly into the parking lot where I parked my car this morning.

I parked my Audi next to a red Chevy pick up truck that has a large bumper sticker that reads, "God is all-knowing and all-powerful." From this view, anyone can see straight into the driver's side of my vehicle. *Whose idea was it anyway to issue assigned parking spaces?* It is 12:00 p.m. I must call Mike to let him know that we should meet at 1:00 p.m. instead of noon. *Ring! Ring!* No answer. I look outside my office to question the staff about the window, but the office is empty. *Everyone is trying to beat the lunch crowd.*

If I leave the office now, then I can meet Mike by 1:00 p.m. *Where is my coat?* I am sure I brought it in this morning. Let me check Christy's station. No, it is not there. I must have left it in my car. *Where are my car keys?* Startled, I hear someone walk up behind me.

"Hi, Rebecca," Jimmy says.

"You won't believe this, Jimmy, but I can't find my coat or my car keys."

He looks at me and says, "Maybe I can help you look in your office." Before I can respond, Jimmy forces his way into my office.

The way he is looking at me makes me uneasy. *There is something different about his eyes.* I take a deep breath and say, "No thanks, I can find them." As I start to head for the door, he quickly slides his foot out, causing me to fall. He uses his arm to push the door shut while shoving his knee in my back. I attempt to let out a scream but the weight of his leg on my back stifles my sounds. I am convinced this is not happening. This can't be happening. *Where is everyone?*

He reaches into his pocket and takes out a sharp blade and places the blade to my throat. I try pushing him off of me, but my body collapses to the floor. *My shoe!* If I can bring my leg up toward me, then I can grab my shoe and defend myself. *Smart man!* Jimmy uses the back of his heel to push both shoes off my feet and turns me around to face him. *Help! Help!* A sharp pain is shooting down my right temple, and my arms feel like they are broken.

Try to reason with him. "No! Wait, Jimmy, you don't have to do this. Please, don't do this." Jimmy looks at me with cold black eyes that hold my gaze for only a second. I black out, thinking about all that has happened that morning. Mike, he is expecting me at the Deli. He will stop by the office if I am not there. Christy, she must be back from lunch. I need to discuss financial matters with her.

My voice disappears, along with my will to live. *Do you hear that?* The window springs open, and a soft breeze enters the room. Jimmy jumps up to shut the window. I grab my paperweight off my desk, and with all my might, I hit him across his mouth. I lunge for the door, pushing his upper body away from me with my foot. He looks like he is fighting someone, but with whom? He looks like he is losing the fight, but with whom?

Oh my God, can it be? I turn around to see Jimmy face down on the floor, unable to move. I run down the hall, past the receptionist's desk to the only safe place I know. *A corner spot in the back of my closet.* I reach up and find my coat hanging untouched where I had left it, with my keys and cell phone in the left pocket. I dial 911 and begin to report a rape.

Knock, Knock! "Ms. Rebecca, it's me Christy. Please, open the door."

"No! Go away," I tell her.

"The police are here. They want to talk to you." *Where is my strength? How do I lift myself up off the floor? How do I explain what just happened?*

"No, I won't come out." I hear the officer's voice telling me that everything is going to be all right. *How does he know?* The officer says that they have arrested Jimmy McDowell and need me to release a statement. Shaking back and forth, my breath becomes faint and my eyes swollen from crying. *God help me!* I reach up to turn the doorknob when a cool breeze brushes against my hand. At that moment, I know that God is with me.

I release my statement to the officer, and Christy walks me to the ambulance. *My assignment was for me to help her, and here she is helping me.* Christy says that she will ride with me to the hospital and is happy that I am all right. Somehow her words do not register, because my mind is still playing back that horrible movie. "Thanks," I say. With tears in my eyes, I look up at my office window *only* to see that the window is closed shut.

What is the lesson?
God is power!

Are you aware of your surroundings at all times? In this story, we see that Rebecca, who works at Thomas and Thomas Associates, encounters sexual abuse on her job. Rebecca is portrayed as a confident individual who enjoys life. The story states that she walks with her head held high and her face gleams with expectation. Although Rebecca's demeanor is one of calmness, her spiritual faith needs nourishing. We should never doubt God's ability but always have faith (John 20:24–28).

In the story, we see that Rebecca is troubled by the open window but simply ignores the warning signs. The first time the window opens, the guard appears, saying that he has taken it upon himself to close the window. Do you see anything wrong with this picture? We should never trespass on another's private property, nor force ourselves on anyone. Aggressive behavior can lead to abuse, causing grief for the victim and the family (Genesis 34:1–2, 7).

The second time the window opens, Rebecca notices a bumper sticker that reads, "God is all-knowing and all-powerful" (Psalm 139:1–3). Do you believe that God can show up in your situation and make you whole again?

The third time the window opens, Rebecca escapes the guard, and God's presence is manifested (Genesis 32:24–29). How many times will it take for God to get your attention?

Although Rebecca is nice to the guard unknowingly, she is not beyond help. God shows up when she least expects it. We should be glad to know that God is always present. We see in the story that Rebecca runs to her closet for protection. God can show up even in the closet. He will hold your hand and minister words of encouragement right where you are (Acts 5:17–20).

God allows us to go through certain trials in order to increase our faith. If we never go through anything, then how will we know that he can heal, deliver, and comfort us? God will cause your enemies to suffer for any wrongdoing (2 Kings 17:39). So don't give up. God loves you, and he wants you to be safe.

Chapter XII
"Mission Accomplished"

Home

Shining bright across the room, I see a burst of light. What appears as a single source of light is *now* a multitude of others. I move in closer for a better look and notice they form a pathway. The desire to see what lies ahead makes my decision that much easier. With each step, I am thankful to God for giving me a life that is fulfilling. It hurts to recall the priceless moments shared with family and friends. *Don't leave them now without a word or explanation.* I look around, unsure of my tomorrow. Then, out of nowhere, an overwhelming peace comes that forcibly takes over. I want to stay on the well-lit path to see my Heavenly Father. God has called me home to be a part of his glorious kingdom—a place where praise and worship never ceases. My work on earth is complete, and this is the time for me to go. I wonder how many people God has called home on this beautiful day.

Revelation 21:5: "And he that sat upon the throne said, Behold, I make all things new. And he said unto me, Write: for these words are true and faithful."

Funeral Procession

One year ago, I said goodbye to a very dear friend. I promised to never forget the times we spent laughing. I cried that day when the pastor announced, "Please stand for the final prayer." As the time grew near to leave the church, I dreaded going to the burial. That day it rained, and the casket glistened with flowers. Again I cried as the body was lowered deep into the ground. Hands reached out to steady my walk as I proceeded to my car. The long ride home was forever daunting and seemed so far. Alone in my room, I tried to make sense of a life that was suddenly gone. No words can describe my feelings of loneliness and loss. In my heart, I knew that the memories would always remain, but my mind wouldn't move past the hurt and pain. Then one night in prayer, God spoke to me and said, "Fear not my child; his life is in now in my hands. His journey is over, but you must move on ahead. Live out your purpose to save lost souls on my behalf."

> **Matthew 25:21:** "His lord said unto him, Well done, thou good and faithful servant: thou hast been faithful over a few things, I will make thee ruler over many things: enter thou into the joy of thy lord."

All Aboard!

Moving at full speed, straight ahead, the whistle blows. The wheels are turning, and the conductor yells, "All clear." The train stops, and my mind wanders. *Where is this train going?* "All aboard," the conductor says. Giddy with excitement, I can barely stand. The train I am on is the overnight express. My bags are heavy, so I quickly find a seat. I look around at others to see who I will meet. There are two, maybe three interesting folks, but the others I see don't measure up. "Tickets, please," the man shouts from behind. I look at his demeanor and immediately frown. He looks worn, beaten, and bruised. Life must be hard; I can tell by his shoes. "Did you say something?" he asks.

"Oh no," I reply. "I was just sitting here wasting time."

"Good day to you," he says with a smile. I look in my seat and find a gold coin. He must have dropped this out of his pocket. "Hey sir. Hey sir, I have something of yours." I reach for his shoulder, and then he is gone. *Where did he say this train was going?* I turn around to see no one aboard, so I reach for my bags, but they are gone. The train is still moving, and the coin is still here. "Last stop," the conductor says and then sounds the horn. I get off the train slowly to see a parade of people marching in the street. The train has arrived at a familiar place—a place called glory and eternal rest.

Revelation 21:4: "And God shall wipe away all tears from their eyes; and there shall be no more death, neither sorrow, nor crying, neither shall there be any more pain: for the former things are passed away."

House Fire

The bright orange blaze leaps to the top of the roof, leaving nothing to the imagination. People standing by watch as the flames engulf the side of the house. The fire has reshaped the exterior siding to a mere charcoal cloud. "Help! Help!" Screams are heard from the shadows trapped inside the home. "Somebody please call 911!" shouts a neighbor, who desperately tries to break down the front door. The black smoke that pours out of the third-floor window is thick and steady. *There is nothing to do but pray.*

The fire spreads quickly, claiming lives that are too young to leave this place. As swift movements are detected in the house, the desperation to save one life becomes urgent. The neighbor gathers a few wet blankets and towels and then motions for the crowd to lend him a hand. With the weight of four guys pushing against the door, the hinges loosen, and the door falls to the ground. The neighbor covers himself in the blanket and proceeds to search all areas of the home.

"I'm coming!" he yells into the musty air. The echo of his words bounces off the exposed framework. He reaches the dark hallway while inhaling fumes and swallowing the taste of death. *Where is the fire department?* The neighbor watches as the flames begin to move up the blanket, taunting him to abandon his mission. "I'm coming!" he yells. The staircase now ablaze, the neighbor runs toward the back of the house. Tightly clutching the towel in his hand, he says a prayer and gazes at the vacant shell around him. *Nowhere to go!* The neighbor reflects on how the kitchen that once used to bake cakes and pies now resembles a space where time and destiny have chosen to congregate.

He can hear crying voices bleeding through the walls as the heat intensifies. *Crash!* Helpless, the neighbor shields his face from the shattered glass caused by the explosion. *1905 Cederway Drive!* Sirens are heard from fire engines racing up the street to suppress the fiery blaze. "Any survivors?" The policeman asks. "Not on this side," a man responds. "This was a Christian home. They were all safe in life or death. These warriors have transitioned to their new home."

What is the lesson?
God is Alpha and Omega!

Death is certain! Are you saved? In the story, we see a neighbor risk his life to save people inside a burning home. Step by step, the reader is taken through the last accounts of the neighbor's noble attempt to save lives. We watch as the neighbor frantically calls out to the family, who gives no response (Luke 12:39–40).

As the heat intensifies, we see that the flames in the kitchen trap the neighbor. The kitchen is symbolic of the neighbor's spiritual revelation. This is shown when he states that time and destiny have chosen to congregate (Ephesians 1:17–18).

After the explosion, we see that the fire department arrives, searching for survivors. A man replies, "Not on this side," suggesting that everyone involved is now safe in heaven (Genesis 1:1, 8–9). Is heaven your home? If you die today, where will you spend eternity?

God is salvation. God is peaceful and just. God is merciful and omnipotent. God is faithful and sovereign. God is loving and courageous. God is truth and power. God is the beginning and the end (Revelation 22:12–13). God forgives all sins if you repent and believe in his word. God loves his children unconditionally. He is the same yesterday, today, and forevermore (Hebrews 13:8). One day your journey will come to an end, and wouldn't you like to hear the Master say, "Well done"?

About the Author

Dawn M. Johnson is a resident of Edgewood, Maryland. She obtained her undergraduate degrees from Coppin State University in mathematics and the University of Maryland, Baltimore County, in chemical engineering. She obtained her Master's degree from the University of Phoenix in computer information systems. She currently works as an engineer of the Baltimore City Department of Public Works and enjoys helping others. She has three lovely kids and a wonderful, supportive husband.

Printed in the United States
216401BV00001B/11/P